Professional Pharmaceutical Selling

Jane Williams

Principle Publications, Inc.
Arlington, Texas

Professional Pharmaceutical Selling

ISBN: 0-9704153-7-0
Editor: Lorraine Griffin
Cover Design: GRIFFININSPIRED.COM

Library of Congress Control Number: 2005928761

Published in the United States of America.

Questions may be directed to:

Principle Publications, Inc.
4101 W. Green Oaks Blvd.
Suite 305-585
Arlington, TX 76016
principlepublications.com

Praise for Jane Williams'

Insider's Guide to the World of Pharmaceutical Sales

Professional Reviews:

"*The Insiders Guide to the World of Pharmaceutical Sales* by Jane Williams is the premier resource for professionals considering a sales career in the pharmaceutical industry. The book serves as a wonderful road map and prepares job seekers for the highly competitive and intensive interview process used by leading pharmaceutical companies. As the Director of Alumni Career Services at the University of Southern California serving over 200,000 alumni, I recommend this book to our alumni interested in pharmaceutical sales. I compare Ms. William's book now in it's 8th edition to the bestselling job-hunting book 'What Color Is Your Parachute' by leading career guru Richard Nelson Bolles. The *Insider's Guide to the World of Pharmaceutical Sales* is among the top career guides on the market.

Thank you Ms. Williams for this invaluable career resource."

Lori Shreve Blake, Director
Alumni & Student Career Services
University of Southern California

"Jane Williams' fabulous book, 'Insider's Guide to the World of Pharmaceutical Sales' ... is a MUST-READ for any resume writer who works with individuals wanting to get into pharmaceutical sales ..."

Bridget Weide, C.P.R.W.
Editor, Resume Writers' Digest

"Jane Williams has supplied her readers with a power-house of information in an easy to read, concise format. The *Insider's Guide...* is an absolute necessity for anyone seriously considering a career in pharmaceutical sales."

Lorraine Griffin
Editor, Resume Authors

"This is the definitive information and 'how-to' book in this field..."

Lois Jobe, C.P.R.W.
Certified Professional Resume Writer
ASAP Resume Services

More Books
by
Best-Selling Author

Jane Williams

Insider's Guide to the World of Pharmaceutical Sales, 8th Edition
ISBN: 0-9704153-9-7
Pub: 2005

Scheduled for release in July 2005, the 8th Edition of the *Insider's Guide to the World of Pharmaceutical Sales* is expected to exceed sales of the popular 7th Edition of the *Insider's Guide to the World of Pharmaceutical Sales.*

Insider's Guide to the World of Pharmaceutical Sales, 7th Edition
ISBN: 0-9704153-6-2
Pub: 2003

The bestselling pharmaceutical sales interview guide, has been described as the "how to" book for surpassing the competition and landing a pharmaceutical sales position. *Resume Authors* describes it as "...a powerhouse of information...an absolute necessity for anyone seriously considering a career in pharmaceutical sales." In addition to being a favorite among individual pharmaceutical sales job seekers, this book is utilized as a text and teaching tool at universities, colleges, and career offices across the United States.

Insider's Guide to the World of Pharmaceutical Sales, Other Editions:

ISBN: 0-9704153-5-4; 6th Edition, Pub: 2002
ISBN: 0-9704153-4-6; 5th Edition, Pub: 2001
ISBN: 0-9704153-3-8; 4th Edition, Rev. Pub: 2000
ISBN: 0-9704153-2-4; 4th Edition, Pub: 2000
ISBN: 0-9704153-0-3; 3rd Edition, Pub: 1999
2nd Edition, Pub: 1999
1st Edition, Pub: 1998

Sell Yourself: Master the Job Interview Process
ISBN: 0-9704153-8-9
Pub: December, 2004

Sell Yourself contains vital, specific information detailing how to interview successfully. All of the research and industry knowledge in the world will not guarantee anyone a job. The position always goes to the person who excels at self-selling because the best sales person always gets the job.

Look for these titles at local and on-line bookstores.

For more information contact:

Principle Publications, Inc.
4101 W. Green Oaks Blvd., Suite 305-585
Arlington, TX 76016
sales@principlepublications.com

Contents

Author
Preface
Welcome

Part 1

Chapter 1   **You're A Rep! Now What?**   **15**
Overview
Safety

Chapter 2   **Pharmaceutical Sales
Representative**   **19**
Training
Job Responsibility
Performance Analysis and Review

Chapter 3   **Adult Learner**   **37**
Characteristics
Personality Styles

Chapter 4   **Physician Education and
Training**   **43**
Physician Education
Physician Training
Physician Jobs

Chapter 5   **Successful Selling**   **47**
Successful Selling Requirements
Basic Sales Presentation
Detailed Sales Presentation
Sales Call Evaluation

Part 2

Chapter 6   **Office-Based Physicians**   **61**
Relationship Selling
Consultative Selling
Physician Calls
Gatekeeper
Door Openers

Chapter 7   **Hospital-Based**
Physicians and Departments 69
Hospital Sales Calls
Private and Public Hospitals
Hospital Departments
Key Hospital Personnel
Physician Access
Nursing Homes
P&T Committee
Emergency Medicine

Part 3

Chapter 8   **Selling to Pharmacists**   **89**
Pharmacist's Job Description
Omnibus Budget Reconciliation Act
Medication Therapy Management
Pharmacy Sales Calls
Clinical Pharmacists
Hospital Pharmacy Department
Nursing Homes/Institutions
Staff Pharmacists
Pharmacy Consultants
Community Projects

Chapter 9   **Managed Care**   **101**
Managed Care Organizations
Pharmacy Benefit Manager
HMO Variations
Contract Models
Capitation

Selling to MCO Physicians
Prior Authorizations

Conclusion   **113**

Part 4

Resources   **117**

Index   **119**

Author

Jane Williams is a multi-time winner of the coveted pharmaceutical industry President's Club Award, former certified sales trainer, consultant and recognized authority in the pharmaceutical sales industry. She formerly worked for Roche Biomedical and Boehringer Ingelheim Pharmaceuticals.

She has been interviewed several times by such entities as the *Dallas Morning News* and *Selling Power Magazine*. Additionally, she has served as a guest panelist on *HireRx*. Her bestselling book, the *Insider's Guide to the World of Pharmaceutical Sales*, is utilized as a text and teaching tool for sales and marketing classes in universities across the United States and is the featured pharmaceutical sales interview guide on sites such as *job-interview.net*. Because of the phenomenal success of the *Insider's Guide*, Ms. Williams receives frequent requests for seminars and speaking engagements.

Building upon her success in offering a comprehensive bestselling job interview guide for those aspiring to a pharmaceutical sales career, Ms. Williams has written a job interview guide that teaches interviewees to sell themselves during job interviews of all types. That title, *Sell Yourself: Master the Job Interview Process* quickly moved to the #1 sales position for "job interview" guides on sites such as *Amazon.com*.

Now, due to high demand from *Insider's Guide* customers, Ms. Williams has written this book, *Professional Pharmaceutical Selling*, a book that provides more in-depth selling help to new pharmaceutical sales representatives.

Preface

The primary purpose of this book is to provide new pharmaceutical sales representatives with additional pharmaceutical, medical, healthcare and selling skills knowledge to increase their ability to excel at selling, achieve faster control of their assigned sales territories and become contributing team members faster.

Additionally, the new pharmaceutical sales representative will find this book to be a handy reference book that may be studied and reviewed between sales calls. Less emphasis is placed on the basic sales presentation because the pharmaceutical employer will provide excellent sales instruction concerning that aspect of the position.

The reader, upon completion of this book, should have a better understanding of the medical industry as it relates to the successful pharmaceutical sales job performance.

While this book provides excellent healthcare and pharmaceutical selling background information, *under no circumstances should it be used as a visual or sales aid during a sales call*. Your company provides approved sales aids and literature to be used during sales presentations to physicians and healthcare workers. The intended use of this book is as a text to be used to study for increased knowledge and understanding relating to the pharmaceutical sales industry.

Welcome!

Gaining a pharmaceutical sales position is exciting and an exceptional accomplishment in itself. This makes you a member of a very elite group of sales professionals. Much will be expected of you. Are you up to the challenge?

Professional Pharmaceutical Selling has been written with the new pharmaceutical sales representative in mind. It is designed to not only help you get through that first crucial year but to help you excel in your first year. You will find information that has taken others significant time to learn; information that you may not be given at all by your prospective employer.

Part

1

Always have a reason for being there.

Chapter 1

You're A Rep!
Now What?

You're a Pharmaceutical Sales Representative! Now what?

You've just survived three to six grueling interviews and you've got the job! At first you simply feel relieved, happy, and very tired. It is only later that fear and anxiety begin to make an appearance into this otherwise happy story with the great ending. Have you bitten off more than you can chew? In any sales job you either "do" or you "die." You've convinced some important people that you can "sell" and now you have to deliver.

First of all, you must know the answers to the following questions:

- What do pharmaceutical sales representatives do?
- How are pharmaceutical sales representatives trained?

- What are the job responsibilities of pharmaceutical sales representatives?
- How do I sell the product to different types of physicians and other medical personnel?
- How do I get my products on hospital/HMO formularies so that my physicians can write prescriptions for my products?

These questions are all answered in the following chapters.

Safety

Your safety must be treated with the necessary precaution. While you should not be overly concerned because being a pharmaceutical sales representative is a very safe job, you must always use good judgement when performing your job as you would with any position.

Be aware of your surroundings at all times. Watch for any type of behavior from individuals that seem out of place. This is especially true when you are retrieving items from the trunk of your car.

Discuss rep safety with your district manager. He or she can give you guidelines for how many days supply of samples and literature you should carry in your car.

Since pharmaceutical sales representatives do not typically carry or leave samples of Schedule II (addictive) drugs, most pharmaceutical sales representatives will work for years, most likely their entire career without having a single incidence of car theft, damage, or any threat to their person. Because the world isn't a perfectly safe place to be and to work, normal safeguards are employed to keep you and your company supplies and samples safe.

Chapter 2

Pharmaceutical Sales Representative

How are pharmaceutical sales representatives trained?

After a sales representative is hired, the representative will be placed immediately in some type of training program. That training program normally consists of all of the following:

- **Home Study.** Usually, the new hire is given anatomy, physiology and pharmacology study materials along with sales materials. The new hire studies for one to two weeks before being tested on the materials. If the new hire makes an acceptable score the new hire is scheduled for the initial training class. If the new hire does not make an acceptable score, a sales

*This chapter, excerpted from the *Insider's Guide to the World of Pharmaceutical Sales,* provides a basic overview of the rep's training and job responsibilities with detailed, new information provided throughout the following chapters.

trainer will work with the new hire to get that person up to speed on the materials.

- **Initial Training.** Initial training class is where the real work begins. This class is extremely difficult! There is an excellent chance that you will work harder than you ever have in any class that you've ever attended. Why? You will not only have to master the anatomy, physiology and pharmacology study materials, and take more tests, but you will have to pass product sales presentations and demonstrate all of the new selling skills that you have learned. Your sales presentations will be taped, reviewed and critiqued. Your strengths and weaknesses will be discovered. Is this stressful? Of course, it is. Is it worth it? You bet it is! The sales trainers will help you become the best pharmaceutical sales representative that you can be, and the **best** earn the most.

- **Sales Meetings.** Sales meetings at all levels usually incorporate sales training classes into the schedule. For example, during district meetings you will present products to your teammates. They will do the same and then everyone discusses these presentations and learns from their team members. New product information is introduced as well as new goals. It's a great learning experience and a very pleasant one.

- **Sales Workshops.** All of the pharmaceutical companies offer mandatory sales workshops for their pharmaceutical sales or territory sales representatives. The purpose of offering the workshops is to keep the sales force in top shape by constantly improving their selling skills.

- **Advanced Sales Classes.** Pharmaceutical sales representatives who show initiative or proficiency in their profession are often encouraged by their company to achieve even better results so the company offers advanced sales classes for them to attend. The advanced sales classes cover a specific selling environment such as the hospital, specialty area, government or managed care selling environments. These classes are designed to further enhance the selling skills of those pharmaceutical sales representatives who have been selected for promotions into advanced sales positions.

Typical Day.

Pharmaceutical sales representatives meet with physicians through preset appointments and through "cold" calls, unscheduled meetings with physicians. During these calls, the sales representative will present information on a company specific product following the guidelines established and approved by the pharmaceutical sales employer. On an average day a pharmaceutical sales representative will:

- Present their product to 8-10 "office-based" and/ or "hospital-based" physicians.

21

- Average two (2) pharmacy calls (sales presentations to pharmacists) per day.
- Average one (1) hospital call (sales presentations to physicians, key medical personnel, and pharmacists) per day in some territories.

Product Presentation.

Product presentations are the primary sales responsibility in a pharmaceutical sales representative's job description. During a product presentation a pharmaceutical representative will:

- Open a product discussion by making an attention-getting statement or asking a question.
- Describe or paint word pictures of patient types and disease states so that the physician will identify with the presentation message.
- Explain how your medication will benefit the patient AND the physician.
- Supply an indication, mechanism of action, contraindications, side effects and dosing information for the product.
- Overcome objections or simply supply additional information through the use of proof sources such as medical studies and visual aids.
- Present cost-effectiveness and therapeutic advantage information. This is important and a concept that has proven very effective over the past several years as compared to just covering efficacy and side effects as was emphasized in the past.
- Ask for the business and gain a commitment from the physician to write prescriptions and/or start patients on the product with samples supplied by you.

- Follow-up on all sales calls with another sales call with the goal of advancing the sale every time.

Proof Source.

Proof sources are written documents that prove claims you have made. Proof sources commonly used by pharmaceutical sales representatives are:
- pharmaceutical company "visuals"
- pharmaceutical product studies
- sales aids

Product Knowledge.

The sales representatives are responsible for knowing and staying current on their company's products and information, as well as knowing and staying current on the competitor's products and information. This goal is accomplished by: company meetings, classes, mailings, literature, e-mails and voice mail messages. These are all part of an educational package provided by the pharmaceutical company to keep the sales representative's product and competitive knowledge current.

Organize territory.

There are different methods used to organize territories based upon the company's plan of action. Some methods include:

- **Call Planner**. This varies from company to company, but basically it is a list of the physicians in the representative's territory. The company will rank the physicians based on the pharmaceutical company's knowledge of the physicians' specialties, prescribing habits, and potential to write prescriptions for your product. This helps the representative to know where time would be best spent.

- **Territory Analysis**. Companies may provide most of the information for a territory analysis. The representative may also be required to access information for this analysis. This analysis will cover geography and different medical institutions, as well as different physicians in a specific area.

- **Future Projects And Products**. Based on company information, decisions about calling on different institutions, physicians and pharmacists, etc. will be based on what is in the "pipeline." **The "pipeline" refers to research projects and developmental pharmaceutical products.**

Prioritize Activity.

Where should the representative work? What should the call frequency be?

The territory location, district manager, and representative's knowledge will determine where one should spend most of one's time. Basically, the representative uses the company resources available to determine where the business is in the territory. The pharmaceutical company will determine the targeted physician's potential to write prescriptions for the company's products. This information helps create the sales representative's call planner. In other words, this information tells the new pharmaceutical sales representative which physicians should be called upon.

Call frequency is determined by the territory analysis. Your district manager will be very helpful in providing the necessary information for this decision. All pharmaceutical companies have a sales plan of action and sales goals that help determine where a pharmaceutical sales representative will work. This information also determines how often the pharmaceutical sales representative will call upon targeted customers. How often physicians are called upon is determined by their potential, their actual writing habits and accessibility.

Which projects should gain priority?

Based on the current plan of action and future forecasts, you will be able to decide along with your district manager which projects should be completed first.

Continuing Education.

All major pharmaceutical companies offer assistance to their employees in regard to continuing education. Most have in house on-going CE (continuing education) programs that are product and company specific. These are necessary to keep the representatives up to date on their products and to sharpen those very necessary selling skills.

When sales representatives are hired by pharmaceutical companies, they are all given pharmacology and anatomy information to learn. They are also given specific product and disease state information to learn. Each company has an "initial training" session where the new hires are evaluated, tested and coached on how to sell. During the course of the sales representatives' tenure with the company they will have ample opportunity to attend advanced, continuing education classes through their employer to keep sales knowledge and selling skills up to date.

Most companies also encourage and support the employees desire to further their formal education. Many will offer reimbursement of fees paid in the pursuit of an acceptable advanced degree from an accredited college/university.

Medical Research.

Different ways to stay current on information:

- **Company provided literature**. Meetings will be held at regular intervals and these are called **POAs or "plan of action"** meetings. New sales literature including visual aids, studies, article reprints and various selling aides are introduced at these meetings.

- **Internet-medical literature search**. In addition to company provided literature and aids, one may also surf the net for medical literature. *This literature must always be for your information only!* Companies have strict policies about the use of literature. No literature may be used on the job without your company's approval. There are valid, legal reasons for this. Always follow your company's policy!

- **Medical Library**. This is one of the oldest methods of acquiring medical information. Any major hospital will have a reasonably sized library and relevant information can be obtained there.

- **Medical Journals**. Medical Journals are excellent sources of information. They present current opinions from the leading medical experts on various disease states and treatment options. The latest studies will be published in these journals. Ads for new and soon to be released products can also be found in these journals.

- **Specialists (M.D.s) involved in research**. In larger areas/cities, there are usually specialists involved in medical research. They will often be found at medical schools, but may also be out in the private practice area. These specialists are a great source of information. After all, they perform the testing and do the necessary research for new products. They know what will be available before anyone else outside the pharmaceutical industry.

Medical Community News.

In addition to medical information, there is always other news...personal news as well as professional news:

- **Hold shared, personal information sacred!**
As soon as you start to work in your territory,
you will become knowledgeable about private/
personal information. You are honor bound to
keep such information private. Your reputa-
tion and credibility require that you protect the
privacy of your customers and their patients.
This doesn't mean that you should not report
activity that you believe is harmful or illegal.
This refers to keeping physician confidences.
These are very often personal and have nothing to do with the practice of medicine.

- **Being tactful and considerate of your physicians requires more than polite behavior.**
After you become a pharmaceutical sales representative, there are basic guidelines which
sales representatives are expected to adhere
to while in the field. Every company is different. Every pharmaceutical company will train
their representatives and cover office etiquette
with the representative. Basically, keeping in
mind that the physicians' offices are like
homes, places this situation in perspective.
You wouldn't enter someone's home, rush to
the back, hide, and pounce on the homeowner,
would you? Of course not! While being assertive can pay huge dividends, being "pushy"
can get you pushed out the door and told not
to return. Learn the office environment; get to
know the people before you decide which approach is best to gain time with the physician.

Attend Company Meetings.

Every company has different types of meetings that the pharmaceutical sales representative attends. These are:

- **POA Meetings.** POA stands for "plan of action." These are the normal meetings that may be held at the district, regional, or national level. At these meetings the company will share with the representatives what the marketing plan will be for the next three to four month period. *Certain product features and benefits will be the major focus for product marketing.* Features describe your product. Benefits explain the advantage of the product feature to the physician and the patient. Everything is explained in detail and everyone is taught to present the information correctly and effectively at these meetings.

- **National Meetings.** These meetings are held once a year or once every two years, depending upon the company. They are usually working meetings. Many will incorporate a POA with a new product launch meeting. Quite often, news about the company and achievement awards is on the agenda. These meetings present opportunities to network within the pharmaceutical company.

- **Regional/Bi-Regional Meetings.** These can be POA, product launch, achievement awards, etc. meetings just as the others can.

- **District Meetings**. Most POA meetings will be held at this level. Other special meetings will be called to meet the needs of the particular district to which you belong. While individual efforts are absolutely necessary for your personal success and the success of your district, region, and company, **teamwork is a key component to the district and company's success**.

- **President's Club/Circle Meetings**. These type meetings are usually reserved for award winners and are quite special. They are usually held in vacation settings. All expense paid trips for you and your significant other to beautiful places are part of the reward for a job well done.

- **Educational Meetings**. Not only are there opportunities to continue your education within the company, there are many opportunities outside your company. These include attending medical seminars, pharmaceutical representative meetings, speaker programs and various other meetings within the medical community.

- **Performance Meetings**. Generally these are one on one meetings with your district manager to assess your progress. These are very valuable meetings because they highlight good performances, find areas for improvement and set future goals. Performance meetings are dedicated to helping sales representatives achieve their highest potential.

Medical Meetings.

As an employee of a pharmaceutical company, you have to be present at various medical meetings which focus on physician education, rather than the pharmaceutical sales representative's education. Supporting CE (continuing education) for physicians occurs in different ways:

- **Medical Society Meetings**. Pharmaceutical sales companies often call upon their sales representatives to attend medical meetings. At this type of meeting, representatives normally set up "displays." This is literally a display of current company-approved literature and products. During breaks between listening to experts speak on current areas/problems in medicine, physicians will walk up to the displays to speak with representatives in order to gain current product information.

- **Dinner/Lunch Speaker Programs**. Usually, a representative will either ask a specialist in their territory or a specialist who speaks nationally to speak to a local medical society. The medical society and the district manager approve these programs. The representative will coordinate everything including speaker's fees, accommodations, program location, guest list, dinner menu and invitations.

- **Journal Club Meetings**. Sometimes the only way to see some busy hospital physicians, or perhaps even office-based physicians, is to get invited to journal club meetings. At these meetings, one physician (they take turns) will present a paper of interest to the group. The entire group will have a "brain storming" session. This is just another way that physicians keep up with current therapy in the medical field. Doing your homework and finding out who the members are will help you know where to go to offer your assistance to the group. ***Remember that these are not pharmaceutical sales representative meetings!*** These are physicians' meetings. You must offer useful information if you are to be considered a valuable resource to the group. These meetings offer a great opportunity to develop rapport with important physicians.

Gain Formulary Acceptance.

In addition to calling on office-based physicians, it is very often necessary to call on pharmacy directors and clinical pharmacists in hospitals as well.

Most companies will have "Medical Specialists." These are experienced, "top-performing" pharmaceutical sales representatives who only work within hospitals and large clinics. Sometimes, there are areas where an "office-based" or "field" pharmaceutical sales representative can help the medical specialist. During product launches in particular, extra help is needed to gain enough time with key people. Pharmacy directors, as well as key physicians determine whether your product is placed on the formulary at the hospital. If the product is on the formulary, then the physicians can prescribe it for their hospital patients. If the product isn't on the formulary, then the physicians can't prescribe it for their hospital patients without tremendous difficulty, or perhaps not at all. This is very important! It affects your ability to promote your product inside the hospital and outside the hospital. Product formulary acceptance usually takes teamwork.

Educational Meetings.

Not only do representatives attend the above-mentioned medical meetings, quite often they organize them. Physicians soon learn whom they can depend on for help. That person needs to be YOU! Even though this may sometimes be considered "above and beyond" your job description, the more helpful you are to your customers, the more they will appreciate your efforts. This brings many rewards. This can also gain you entrance to previously private areas of the physician's world. Representatives can be barred from many areas and this increases the difficulty of doing your job. Good communication skills and good problem solving skills can help ensure that you are one of the successful representatives who are welcome in areas where others are not.

Learning Programs.

Work with medical leaders. There are other types of learning programs such as tele, audio and video conferences. Many hospitals enjoy having these educational programs for their physicians. This allows the physicians to earn CEUs (continuing education units) during a luncheon and there is no need for the physicians to take time off work. These programs are usually held in a conference room at the hospital. These "speaker programs" are set up so that physicians across the country can all attend without leaving their home, office or hospital. This can be especially helpful for the public hospital physicians.

Co-Promote Products.

Co-promotion of products within your company or with sales partners from other companies is very common. Sometimes two and even three sales forces within the same company will promote the same product. Sometimes two different companies join forces to promote products to increase coverage of their physician targets without hiring a new sales force. Each sales force will have different, or possibly identical goals. The representatives are given lists of targeted physicians and the names of their sales "partners" who share/overlap their territories. The reason pharmaceutical sales companies want several people calling on the same physician is that the physician will hear the sales message more often. Research indicates that the more the physician hears the message, the more likely he/she is to remember the message and "buy in" if the message is a good one. Research has shown that pharmaceutical sales companies sell much greater quantities of their products by utilizing this repetitive tactic. Representatives make an itinerary that is shared by the pharmaceutical sales partners so that the physician calls can be spaced appropriately. This prevents all the sales representatives who call on a certain physician from showing up the same week and even on the same day. This also allows the representatives to set up in-services and speaker programs as either joint or separate programs that do not interfere with their sales partner's activities.

Assessing Performance.

Every pharmaceutical company will have an assessment program in place to evaluate your performance. Based on this evaluation, you will be guided by your district manager to improve your current sales performance. This also allows you to be recognized and rewarded for superior performance. Everyone needs some method of evaluating progress in order to plan successful sales strategies. The following type of evaluation is commonly used within the pharmaceutical sales industry, as well as other sales industries:

- Performance Evaluation: Designed to maximize your sales performance.

  Major Areas: Examples listed below are areas of responsibility for pharmaceutical sales representatives.

    Sales Performance
    Territory Management
    Selling Skills
    Product Knowledge
    Team Support
    Administration
    Professional/Personal Development

  Objectives: Goals that are attainable, realistic, and applicable.

Dimensions: These are the skills or behaviors that allow you to achieve your goals/objectives.

> Sales Ability/ Persuasiveness
> Planning & Organization
> Analysis
> Innovation
> Teamwork

Tracking Source (Proof): Using the STAR components of situation/task, action and results, you can track your dimensions to see if your objectives are being met.

Tracking Frequency: You will set a tracking frequency to evaluate data based on your methods of tracking and district manager guidelines.

Actual Results: The actual results of your actions. For example, you sold 3.0 million dollars worth of products in your territory exceeding your goal/ objective of 2.5 million dollars. Your current national sales rank is 10 out of 3,500 sales representatives.

Rating: Your rating based on your performance in each key area.

- DM Feedback: District Manager feedback will reflect the feedback given in your performance management documentation.

- Self-Assessment: You will evaluate your own performance and make adjustments to improve your performance.

Chapter 3

Adult Learner

Regardless of whether you are selling to physicians, pharmacists, nurses, or other key medical personnel, they all have one characteristic in common: They are all adults. It is vital to understand how adults learn. Knowing and utilizing this information will help you in your sales calls.

There are four basic commonly accepted personality types that you will encounter while interacting with your customers and these four basic personality types apply to all of us. Many people have written about the same information and have assigned different names to these personalty types. My first exposure to the study and utilization of personality styles and adult learning characteristics in selling situations was through sales training class with Boehringer Ingelheim Pharmaceuticals who utilized the *I-Speak Your Language Manual* published by DBM Publishing in 1993.

Adult Learner Characteristics:

- Adults are motivated to learn by need. If they do not understand the need to learn, they will not do so.
- Adults need to understand why they must learn the material. This allows them to compare the benefits of learning versus the consequences of not learning.
- Adults learn from performing the activity rather than through passive means such as merely listening to a lecturer. This form of learning is also referred to as tactile or kinesthetic learning.
- Adults prefer varied and multiple teaching methods.
- Adults excel at learning based on real-life experiences. This allows relationship learning.
- Adults learn best in informal environments.
- Adults learn best when they participate in dialogue with the instructor.
- Adults need verbal guidance and praise.
- Adults are normally self-motivated and will strive to get the most out of their class/training.
- Adults tend to gather specific information for problem solving versus general information.
- Adults access and use information in a practical manner. They will use the information to relate it to their job or real world experience.
- Adults demand knowledgeable, mature instructors who know their subject matter and how to present it.
- Adult learners have varied educational and work history backgrounds and this must always be considered when relaying information to any particular group.

- 80% of what we learn, we learn through sight.
- We remember 90+% of what we learn when we speak and act.
- We remember things that are repeated.
- We learn best in low-stress environments.
- Adults learn what they have been told and shown how to do and have been allowed to do.
- Instructors should show excitement about learning material.
- Instructors should encourage healthy competition.
- Instructors should give adults choices.

Understanding Adult Personality Styles:

There are four basic personality types that you will encounter while calling on physicians and these four basic personality types apply to all of us. Everyone will have personality characteristics of at least two of these groups. When listing certain physician personality types, I have relied upon my sales training and my personal call experience to identify the types of physician specialities you can expect to find in the four personality groups. These four basic personality types are:

- Thinker: To earn the trust of a thinker you must be thorough, comprehensive, accurate, organized, logical, knowledgeable, use proof sources, and most definitely know the facts about the information you are presenting. When stressed, thinkers tend to act in an "impersonal" fashion causing them to appear "cold" and "uncaring." ALL physicians will be thinkers.

- Feeler: To earn the trust of a feeler you must be honest, personable, maintain eye contact, show a genuine interest in the person, and have a "non-salesperson" manner. You must be warm and friendly. You must talk with them about how their peers feel about the information you have presented, and how using this information helps people. Feelers enjoy casual conversations. When placed under stress they tend to have a "thin skin" and react very emotionally and erratically. Based on my personal experience, I believe you will find that pediatricians, and family practice physicians tend to fall into this category most often.

- Sensor: To earn trust with a sensor, you must have a direct, "to-the-point" approach. You cannot vacillate. You must state your main points briefly and clearly. Avoid being wordy. In other words, just "net it out" or get to the point and get there quickly! Be confident, but do not be pushy. Be assertive. Don't be aggressive. This will win the sensor's respect. Sensors are serious people. Sensors tend to be turned off by emotional comments. Sensors are very punctual. Sensors like to hear both sides of a story, good and bad. When under stress, sensors tend to demonstrate "tunnel vision", bias, and total insensitivity to the feelings of others. Many physician specialists such as neurologists, cardiologists, surgeons, etc. will fall into this category.

- Intuitor: To earn trust with an intuitor you have to "show and tell." Demonstrate the latest and the best, the most innovative way to do whatever you are discussing. Be forward looking. Make the conversation exciting. Intuitors like personable people just like feelers do. Intuitors are innovative thinkers. They look to the future. The more word pictures you paint, the more metaphors you use with an intuitor, the better the impression you will make. Intuitors may appear to be egocentric. When operating under stress they may become very rigid and uncompromising. Many "research" and "teaching institution" physicians will fall into this category.

Everyone will have a predominant style that they normally function well with. Under stress, our personality style may stay the same or we may display a different personality style. First, you need to evaluate your own personality style to better understand how you relate to people. Most successful sales representatives will have Feeler/Sensor personalities with some Intuitor and Thinker traits. In other words, they are versatile and adaptable. As you work through your territory and meet your physicians, developing personality profiles on each physician will help you determine which sales approach will be better received by that physician. You would then plan your sales call based on your knowledge of that particular physician's personality. Why? We all respond better to people who reflect our own personality style. Having similar "personalities" creates an instant comfort zone and makes communication easier and much more effective. The net effect is that you are learning to speak your customer's language.

Chapter 4

Physician Education and Training

Understanding How Physicians Are Trained

Typically a physician's education follows this course:

- Enrolls in a pre-med program upon entering college.
- Performs volunteer work at local hospital.
- Applies for medical school during their fourth year of study.
- Completes four year undergraduate degree
- Upon admission acceptance, attends four year medical school program providing classroom and clinical work study. During medical school an emphasis is placed on pathology, pharmacology, anatomy, physiology, biochemistry, histology and

the study of cadavers. Clinical study is provided at local hospitals and clinics.

- During the fourth year of medical school, an application for medical internship is made.
- After completing the fourth year of medical school, the medical student takes the USMLE, United States Medical Licensing Examination, commonly referred to as the "medical boards" given by the National Board of Medical Examiners. They may also take the FSMB, Federation of State Medical Boards at that time. Medical degrees are granted to those who pass their USMLE exam.

Physicians have the following training:

- Four years of medical school
  Typically, the first two years are devoted to classroom studies and the second two are more heavily devoted to clinical experience and study-internship.
- Internship. Rotating internships provide broad based knowledge of all major medical fields and assist the intern in selecting a residency program for specialization.
- Three years of residency to become primary care physicians. Primary care physicians are Family Practice (FP) and Internal Medicine Physicians (IM).
- Four years (add one year) of residency for Geriatric Specialists.
- Five years (add two years) of residency for Other Specialists.
- All of this training has occurred within a strictly controlled environment.

- On-going continuing education classes and training throughout the physician's career.

Residents compensation:

- Receive three free meals daily.
- Money to partially cover books and conference expenses.
- Receive a pay range of approximately $35,000-$48,000 per year.

Changing methods of teaching and training for physicians:

- Changes to the maximum shift times an intern or resident may be required to work; the amount of time an intern or resident may work without sufficient time off to rest and receive adequate sleep has been reduced for both the patients and the residents safety and well being.
- New teaching programs provide extra help to residents in their teaching roles as mentors to interns and medical students.

Jobs available to physicians:

- Private Practice
  Individual
  Group/Clinic

- University/Hospital-Based Physician
  Private
  State/Federal

- HMO Physician

- Government Physician
  State/Federal Institutions

- Research Physician
  Private
  Federal

- Pharmaceutical Industry Physician
  Research
  Medical Department
  Medical Liaison

The Goal:

"Balance professionalism with humanism,"
according to Harvard Medical School.

Chapter 5

Successful Selling

Successful selling requires the salesperson to:

- Uncover Customer Needs: What is the customer's need? The customer's need is the customer's "want" that can be satisfied by your product. The more needs you can uncover, the more likely you are to have a successful sales call because needs represent opportunities to sell your products. Good listening and probing skills must be used in order to uncover the customer's needs.

- Satisfy Customer Needs: In order to satisfy customer needs, you must understand the need and know how to meet the need. After you clearly understand the need, you will use features and benefits of your products to meet the needs of your customers.

- Recognize Sales Opportunities: What is a sales opportunity? It's a customer problem/need that can be corrected/met by your product.

- Probe Successfully: In order to meet customer needs you must understand what those needs are. Therefore, you must ask smart questions to gather the information that you need to proceed with the sales presentation.

- Offer Support: Offer product benefits to meet your customer's needs.

- Close: Gain a commitment from your customer to purchase your product which you have established will meet your customer's need.

While your employer will send you through a series of company training sessions, this will be much easier and less stressful if you know what to expect. First I will outline the basic parts of the sales presentation. Then we will cover all of the different parts of the sales presentation and what you should be doing to make your presentation an exceptional one.

Basic Sales Presentation:

Opening:

- Gains attention and interest. Always strive to make a simple, powerful, opening sentence. Never open with "I'm here to sell you a product", in any form. Just think about how you react to the telemarketers who call you up at your home during dinner and then try to sell you something you don't want and don't need. Remember that your opener must reflect that you are there to help the physician and his patients. They come first. You don't.

- Never be trite. Don't ever ask foolish questions to open dialogue with your physicians. These foolish questions would be something like: "Do you want to reduce your hypertensive patients' blood pressures?"

- Be Brief. Making one simple, powerful, direct point tends to gain the attention of the physician.

- Never mention product up front. Everyone likes a little mystery. If you mention your product up front, the usual result is physician "shutdown." You can see it in their eyes. They already know "all about your product" unless the product is brand new. In order to share new information about your product you must convey the new information to the physician before the "old" product name is mentioned.

Listen:

- Eye Contact. Don't take your eyes off the physician! That doesn't mean that you should stare at anyone. Just focus on the physician so that he knows he has your undivided attention. This shows that you value what the physician is saying. The physician is also more likely to return the show of respect by maintaining eye contact and listening to you if you have listened to him. Listening carefully while maintaining eye contact also allows you to immediately detect any positive or negative body language.

- Correctly interpret physician dialogue.

  > Verbal. You can be certain that you have understood correctly by rephrasing and asking clarifying questions.

  > Non-Verbal. If the physician suddenly appears "uncomfortable," it's time to stop and find out why. Ask if he has a question or concern about something you've just said, etc.

- Rephrase for understanding. Restating what the physician has said serves more than one purpose. It lets the physician know that you are paying attention, and it also lets him know that what he has said is important to you and you want to understand it fully. Additionally, rephrasing for understanding allows you to be certain that you address the correct issues/objections or interpret support correctly.

- Ask clarifying questions. This takes rephrasing a step further. After you have confirmed that you have rephrased what the physician has said, you must ask any additional questions that are necessary to be certain that you have a complete picture of the problem or objection, etc. You have to know where you stand before you can decide how to get to where you want to go.

Present Product:

- Employ accurate verbalization of product information. You must possess a thorough and complete knowledge of your product in order to present it to the physician. This will require hours of your time. Reviewing the PI (prescribing information) on a regular basis will increase your understanding and promote more accurate verbalization of your product information.

- Present material in logical order. As with any presentation, logic and order must be applied for maximum benefit. Material that is presented in an order and a manner that is clear and easy to follow will be received and retained much better than information presented in an erratic manner.

- Verbalize Selling Points appropriately. Know your product's strengths (benefits) and use them to sell the product. Insert appropriate benefits that are matched to your product features. For example, if your blood pressure product is dosed once daily state this and then list the benefits that once daily dosing provides such as "round the clock" blood pressure control and increased patient compliance due to the once daily dosage.

Dramatize Your Message:

- Be descriptive. This is where you "paint the picture." Make the message come alive by describing in detail the type of patient that your product will help. For example, if you are selling an anti-anxiety medication describe the anxious patient to the physician.

- Attach benefits to product features. Always tell the physician how the features of your products can benefit the patient and the physician. Physicians don't write for products because of product features. They write prescriptions for products because of the benefits that those product features provide to the patient and to himself, the physician.

- Involve the physician. Get the physician to participate in the discussion. It's not a discussion if only one person is speaking. When he becomes involved in the discussion, he's really thinking about the product and how it can help his patient. He is now gaining some ownership of the "information" or is preparing to own it.

- Incorporate stories, testimonials, analogies, similes, etc. Everyone remembers a good story. We remember how the characters came alive during the story. We remember what they were like, what they did and why they did it because it was "real" to us. Make it "real" for the physician by giving him real-world feedback on the product. Learning about other physicians' successes with the product is a very valuable selling and "memory" tool. If his fellow physicians, friends and competitors for patients, are getting great results he will certainly want to have the same success stories in his practice.

- Show appropriate enthusiasm. If you aren't excited about the message you're delivering, how can you expect the physician to get excited about your message? Sincere, enthusiastic people are a virtual breath of fresh air to someone who is in the constant company of people who are hurt or ill. When it is obvious to physicians that you are "sold" on your product, selling your product to the physicians will be much easier.

Probe:

- Ask smart questions. Understand open and closed probes. Use open probes to encourage your customer to expand upon their thoughts. The correct key words for encouraging the customer to talk are: who, what, where, when, why, how and tell me. Sometimes, a closed probe is appropriate. One of those times is when you want to confirm the customer's need. You may want the customer to choose between several choices. Whenever you want to limit the customer's response to a "yes" or "no" answer, use a closed probe. Closed probes include keywords: do, does, is, are, have, has, or, and which. Good probing skills are highly associated with successful sales calls.

- Never use trap questions. No one likes to feel like they are on the witness stand and an adversary is questioning them. That situation is upsetting and it does not endear anyone to the person asking the questions. The person being questioned is immediately on guard because they feel like they are being set up and this causes them to distrust the person asking the questions. Physicians are very bright people who have no difficulty understanding when someone is attempting to entrap them. If you ask "trap" questions of your physicians, you will alienate them immediately.

- Do not harass the physician with too many questions. Ask only necessary questions that are needed to determine where the physician is in the buying curve and for clarification purposes. Too many questions will result in physician "shutdown" and call failure.

- Proper questioning leads to increased dialogue with physicians. Asking smart questions uncovers hidden objections and misperceptions. Smart questions allow for accurate analysis of the physician's concerns and needs. Knowing this information allows you to present appropriate information to the physician to meet his needs.

Support:

- Acknowledge the customer's need. When the physician has shared information with you, including objections and negative information, value it. Acknowledge your physician's concerns and then address the concerns. When the physician tells you exactly what he is thinking and it isn't what you would like to hear, see this as the great stride forward that it is. This isn't a problem; it's a selling opportunity. If he trusts you enough to openly express his opinion, you now have a clear understanding of the situation. Now you can use this information and respond to this selling opportunity.

- Supply appropriate benefits. Make sure that your product benefit meets the physician's need or concern.

Handle Objections:

- Explain and Prove

  Reprints. Use appropriate reprints to answer physician's questions and to overcome physician's doubts. Do not read from the reprint. This is very insulting to the physician who is quite capable of reading the material. Movements must be smooth and must not detract from the presentation.

  Visuals. Use the proper section of the visual to make your point and do not read from the visual. Again, movements must be smooth and must not detract from the presentation.

  Knowledge. Your knowledge of the product that you have gained through company literature, training, and through dialogue with other physicians may be used whenever appropriate.

- Refocus and Redirect:

  Qualify the objection. All this means is that you check for understanding by repeating the objection in the form of a question. You have to understand the objection before you can address it.

  Acknowledge the facts. Expect the physician to make good points. Acknowledge "facts" and his right to an opinion. This will help prevent physician "shutdown." Just be certain that you do not negate your position in the process. You need to be able to show him that you are in agreement on certain issues and clarify others where there may be some misunderstanding.

  Apply empathy. Be understanding. The physician's job is a difficult, very complex job and the demands are very high. Be certain that he knows you appreciate this and that you would like to help.

  Use benefits appropriately. Attach the correct product benefit to the product feature.

  Check for acceptance. Make a statement or ask a question that outlines points of agreement between you and the physician. When the physician confirms your statement, close. Ask for the business.

Close:

- Ask for the business. Always ask the physician to make a commitment to write prescriptions for your product. I have always been amazed by the fact that many pharmaceutical sales reps make it through the entire presentation process and then do not ask for the business either directly or indirectly.

- Finalize the Sale. This occurs when you gain a solid commitment to write prescriptions and you check to see if you need to do anything else to assist the physician. Finding out how many patient starter samples he needs, based on the number of patients he has who are candidates for your particular drug, should give you some idea of the number of prescriptions you can expect this physician to write for your product. Gaining a commitment from the physician to write your product for another select group of patients is also a successful close. Anytime, there is an agreement to write prescriptions whether it is for a few patients or many, you have made a successful presentation and have closed properly.

- Advance the Sale. When you do not gain a solid commitment from the physician to write for your product and you gain a commitment from him to consider your product and meet with you again to learn more about the product, this is a form of advancing the sale because you have won more time with the physician. You then have the opportunity to prepare better for your presentation so that you may close successfully during your next call on this physician.

- Include product dosing in the close. Never end a successful close without adding the proper patient dosing. It is very important that your physician prescribe your product properly.

57

Bridge Correctly:
- Use a smooth, logical transition statement between product presentations. Then move on to your next product presentation.

Building Rapport:
- Done on an individual basis.

Preparing for the next Sales Call:

Evaluating the Sales Call: There are different outcomes in sales calls. You must know how to evaluate your sales call if you are to learn from your mistakes and improve your selling skills. These outcomes are:

- Successful Sales Call: With successful sales calls the customer has made a commitment to prescribe your product or has agreed to some action that has the potential for resulting in increased prescribing of your product.

- Accessibility Sales Call: You have been granted the right to meet with the physician again, but no commitment has been made to write your product.

- Sales Call Failure: This covers everything else. If no commitment of any type has been made, you have failed! This isn't the end of the world. We would all like to be 100% successful every time with our sales calls but in the real world that is not likely to happen because many variables affect your selling success. You must view call failure as a learning experience and then do something about it. Prepare better for future success.

Part

2

Be assertive.
Don't be aggressive.

Chapter 6

Office-Based Physicians

Typically, pharmaceutical sales representatives or territory sales representatives and specialty sales representatives call on office-based physicians. The basic sales force or pharmaceutical sales representatives will usually call on primary care physicians and may call on specialists as well. The specialty sales force will call only on specialists.

With the new PhRMA guidelines setting strict rules for what is and is not acceptable sales practice, the pharmaceutical sales force must do what they should have always done and that is sell the product.

Relationship Selling

The pharmaceutical sales representatives calling on primary care physicians will find that they must use relationship selling and partner with the physician in order to be successful in this very competitive marketplace. How do you accomplish this?

In order to partner with the physician and develop a good working relationship, the sales representative must always present important, useful information to the physician at every call. Is this an easy task? No. You must pre-plan every call to accomplish your goal of selling the product and not wasting the physician's time.

When the physician realizes that he can expect you to provide useful information in a concise organized fashion he will see you more readily and will listen more closely to what you have to say. By providing accurate product information that includes the features, benefits, drug interactions and side effects along with patient profiles for proper patient selection, your physician will soon realize that you take your job seriously. By providing compelling clinical study data from a trusted medical journal to prove your product's superior performance over the competition he will learn to trust you because you back up what you say with a credible proof source. Showing integrity and an equal concern for the welfare of his patients will add the final building blocks to your relationship with the physician.

Consultative Selling

The new selling environment resulting from reduced physician access and changing sales guidelines has produced changes in sales force structure and allocation of marketing funds. One of the fastest growing sales forces within the pharmaceutical industry is the specialty sales force. Specialty sales representatives are usually veteran pharmaceutical sales representatives who possess greater product, anatomy and physiology knowledge along with greater sales experience than the pharmaceutical sales representative. They utilize all the components of relationship selling but take it one step further and add consultative selling to their sales armamentarium. The specialty sales representative specializes in a particular therapeutic area or disease state, therefore their knowledge is more extensive in those specialized areas. Because they possess this higher degree of product and disease state knowledge and often have greater access to consultant physicians within their company's medical departments, they typically enjoy a greater degree of trust and rapport with the specialists.

While specialty sales representatives never advise physicians on patient treatment, the physicians do utilize specialty sales representatives who have won their trust and respect as information sources. Physicians will have more in-depth product, disease state and medical affairs discussions with specialty representatives because the specialty sales representatives are better trained and better educated in all the pertinent areas of interest to the physician.

With this increased level of trust and access comes greater responsibility and accountability. The specialty sales representative must spend considerable time learning new product information and staying up to date on any and all information that affects his or her job performance.

Providing accurate information can never be taken lightly. Patients' quality of life and even their survival can be tremendously impacted by information that the sales representatives provide to physicians.

This job is a very important one and while it certainly should be enjoyed, it must always be taken seriously.

Calling On Physicians

You've already studied your company's materials so you know who your targeted physicians are and how often you should call upon them. Now the fun begins! How do you actually get to see these physicians? How do you get to see them as often as your company would like for you to see them? It takes much more effort than simply mapping out a plan as you have already done. Now you have to get the targeted physicians' cooperation in order to actually make the plan work.

Some physicians have inflexible rules for seeing them at their offices. They may require that you schedule an appointment only when you have a new product. Most will allow better access than that. For example, you may be allowed to schedule an appointment once per month and only on the second and third Tuesday of the month. You may be seen only if you bring in lunch for the physician and his entire staff. This is very common. Your company will allow you an in-service budget and you will certainly use it. You just have to be careful to follow your company's guidelines for in-services and providing meals to physicians.

Certain group practices set up appointments with pharmaceutical sales representatives allowing the representatives to schedule an appointment that gives them two hours to set up a "display" in a room with or without food service. The physicians go into the "rep display room" between patients to speak with the pharmaceutical sales representatives. I love this setup! Sometimes you can see all of the physicians in a group during a single sales call. You may see 12 physicians or more during two hours. This can be extremely productive sales time.

Gatekeeper

What is a gatekeeper? That is the person who guards the physician. Sounds ominous, doesn't it? You probably didn't even know that physicians required body guards. Rather than the typical body guard function, it is the physicians' time that is being protected.

Someone, normally the receptionist, nurse, office manager, nurse practitioner, physician's assistant or the physician's spouse, will be the gatekeeper. This person is extremely important to you! Although, the physician may have rules that allow you to see him, if these people decide they don't like you for some reason, they can effectively ban you from the office. Being courteous and considerate of the staff's time is normally sufficient to stay on good terms with them. Sometimes, however, you must go the extra mile and really pull out all the stops to make a good impression on the staff.

Whatever you do, learn the gate-keepers name and use it! This shows you feel that this person is important. Gather background information on her and then remember to ask appropriate questions. Inquire about her child's soccer team playoffs. Ask how the class she is taking is progressing. Representatives are very often seen as interruptions or as nuisances. Ask always. Use charm, tact and diplomacy when speaking with the gatekeeper. Never push to see the physician. You won't win that tug of war! That doesn't mean that you give up on seeing the physician by any means. It simply means you must find a way to see the physician while not alienating his staff as you are accomplishing this task.

Physician Door Openers

OK. You know the office rules for calling on your targeted physician. Maybe those rules are generous and sufficient. Maybe they're not. What do you do when you have limited or no physician access? Find another way to see the important physician.

Your physician will belong to national and local medical societies and will have admitting privileges at some local hospital.

Some suggestions for seeing physicians:

- Find out which societies he belongs to and what his position is within the society. If he is the president of the local medical society, speak with your district manager to find out what additional services your company may offer to the group if you do not know this information. After you know what you can offer, go back to the physician's office with an offer to speak with him about what you can offer to the local medical society. This is an excellent way to meet, speak with, and develop rapport with the difficult to see, important physician. What are examples of educational programs that you may be able to assist his society with?
    1. Speaker Programs
    2. Specialized In-service Programs

3. *Journal Club Meetings
4. Educational Community Projects. Examples are: Well-ness Clinics and Disease Prevention Workshops
5. Medical Inquiry Department Meetings

- After you find out where your physician has admitting privileges, you can find out which departments he works in based on his specialty and patient population demographics. Then you can look into how you may gain call time with him. The following programs are covered in detail in Chapter 7:
    1. Hospital In-services
    2. Video and Teleconferences
    3. Speaker Programs
    4. Displays

Some years ago, pharmaceutical sales representatives were encouraged to socialize with and even infringe upon physicians personal time outside the office. Unfortunately, this method of contacting physicians has lost much of its effectiveness because of the poor judgement displayed by a few pharmaceutical sales representatives who came before you. It has also been the object of criticism with the development of new rules and standards of business conduct set forth by PhRMA for the pharmaceutical sales professional. I must say that I agree with the new rules because the best sales performance will ultimately go to the best sales person and not the person who has the biggest entertainment budget. The new rules also require sales representatives to work much smarter and to be more effective. This is a positive outcome.

*more information in Chapter 7.

I can not recommend noneducational physician contact outside the office. The reason I can't is because I do not believe that it is ethically correct to infringe upon the private lives of your physicians. They deserve time with their families and friends and should not have to deal with work 24 hours a day. Everyone needs time to rest and recuperate. There is sufficient time and opportunity to perform your job during normal business hours and at scheduled events.

Chapter 7

Hospital-Based Physicians & Departments

Most companies will have medical or hospital specialists. These are experienced, top-performing pharmaceutical sales representatives who only work within hospitals and large clinics. Sometimes, there are areas where an office-based or a "territory" pharmaceutical sales representative can help the medical specialist.

During product launches in particular, extra help is needed to gain enough selling time with key people. Product formulary acceptance usually takes teamwork. Pharmacy directors, as well as key physicians determine whether or not your product is placed on the formulary at the hospital. If the product is on the formulary, then the physicians can prescribe it for their hospital patients. If the product isn't on the formulary, then the physicians can't prescribe it for their hospital patients without tremendous difficulty, or perhaps not at all. Product formulary acceptance is critical to successful hospital product sales. Formulary product acceptance affects your ability to promote your product inside the hospital and affects product sales indirectly outside the hospital.

Where you work and how you work will be determined by your company. Your employer will make this determination based on the type of products they sell and the location of targeted physicians and medical personnel who either have the ability to write prescriptions for these products or have influence over those physician prescribers.

Private and Public Hospitals

What's the difference between these two types of hospitals and how does this affect your ability to do your job?

Private Hospitals

Hospitals owned by the private sector are those community hospitals that accept insurance and provide service for a fee. While this is not always true, the private hospitals usually allow a much higher degree of access to sales representatives than do public hospitals. It is also true that most of your hospital business as a territory representative will not be with private hospitals but with public hospitals.

Medical or hospital sales representatives who promote hospital-use drugs only may call on private hospitals as well as public hospitals.

What is a "hospital" drug? This is a product designated for hospital or emergency use only. It is usually administered to the patient by IV or injection. This type of drug would generally not be promoted to office-based physicians.

Public Hospitals

They are precisely what the word implies; publicly owned. Normally, free care, compensated care, or government service related care is given in these hospitals for minimal or no fee to the patient.

Examples of public hospitals:
>Veterans Affairs Hospitals
>State Hospitals
>County Hospitals
>Teaching Hospitals

Medical or hospital sales representatives will definitely call on public hospitals because of the type of care that these facilities provide to patients, which includes clinic care. Public hospitals tend to perform large volume business treating many patients with chronic and acute illnesses.

Very often, patients are admitted to Veterans Administration Hospitals where they may stay for months. In this type of environment, the patient not only needs "hospital drugs" but will also require routine maintenance drugs for treatment of chronic disease states such as hypertension and diabetes. For this reason, it is very important to win formulary approval for your "hospital" drugs and for your "non-hospital" drugs. Under these circumstances, an office-based representative may be called upon to assist the medical representative. Assistance may be given by working with that representative during speaker programs or product displays. The pharmaceutical sales representative, may also make calls on hospital-based physicians and departments solo or assist the hospital sales representative by providing other types of assistance.

What do you do first?

You will find that there are usually very strict rules governing hospital calls, especially if you are a new pharmaceutical sales representative. Why would this be true for new reps versus veterans? After the hospital personnel get to know you, it is entirely possible that you may not have to follow the strict rules that are in place for pharmaceutical sales representatives. Your professional conduct, good judgement and resource value will dictate whether you are extended more access to physicians and hospital departments. Some hospitals may never make rule exceptions for pharmaceutical sales representatives but many will after you earn the right to be given preferential treatment.

Designated Check-In Department: Central Supply

I'll never forget my first call on a hospital. When I was directed to check-in at the Central Supply department in the basement of the hospital, I thought someone had surely made a mistake. No mistake. Sales representatives are sent over to Central Supply or a "neutral" department or the Pharmacy if they're lucky to sign in and state their reason for being in the hospital, and with whom they have an appointment.

You may not appreciate the routine or the rules, but smart representatives abide by the rules. Failure to follow the rules can get you tossed out and banned from the hospital. Try explaining that to your District Manager! Don't be discouraged by the rules. A little time and experience will educate you on how to be successful at hospital sales. Relationship and consultative selling skills couldn't be more important than in this setting.

Who should you see? Which departments should you call on?

After your company has given you instructions on call activity, you will call upon physicians or healthcare personnel in the departments where your products will be utilized. Physicians are located throughout the hospital and work in the various departments in which they specialize.

Which physician specialties would you expect to find in the hospital? You will find cardiologists, pulmonologists, general surgeons, specialty surgeons, neurologists, pediatricians, obstetricians, oncologists etc. Because hospitals provide critical care, you will find all types of physicians there. These physicians will work in different departments based on their medical specialty and their specific area of responsibility within the hospital. Based on areas of responsibility you will find physicians and non-physician prescribers as listed below, typically in public or teaching hospitals.

Physicians:
>   Department Chiefs
>   Staff or Attending physicians
>   P&T Committee Members
>   Residents/Interns
>   Medical Students

Non-Physician Prescribers:
>Physician's Assistants (PA)
>Nurse Practitioners (NP)

Key Hospital Departments:
>Medical Education Department
>Cath Lab
>CCU- Critical Care Unit
>Nursing Department
>Respiratory Therapy
>Medical Services Departments
>>Medicine
>>Pulmonary
>>Neurology
>>Pediatrics, etc.
>>Surgery
>>Anesthesiology
>>Clinic
>>Emergency Medicine
>Pharmacy

Because of the importance of the pharmacy department and the differences between types of pharmacies and their location and function, this information will be covered in Chapter 8, Selling to Pharmacists.

Because sales techniques and in-services for non-physician or department staff often differ from those for physicians, the selling style tends to be different. While you may experience a time crunch when calling upon these departments, usually it is much easier to gain quality time with staff in hospital departments than it is to gain quality time with physicians inside or outside the hospital.

With both physicians and hospital staff, superior product knowledge is necessary for the successful sales representative. However, good business management knowledge is even more important for hospital sales. For that reason additional time and attention must be paid to the cost-effective advantages that your product has over the competition. While this is important to physicians and private patients, adding a hospital department and that department's budget to the mix will require more creativity, research and preparation for your hospital sales calls.

Physician Access

The rules for seeing physicians inside the hospital are very similar to the rules for seeing office-based physicians. First, ask the designated healthcare person or persons inside the department where your targeted physician works about how the physician sees representatives in that hospital department. Follow the rules. You need to get your foot inside the door so that you can start building good relationships with the healthcare workers as well as the physicians.

Sometimes busy private practice physicians who do not see pharmaceutical sales representatives inside their offices will see representatives at their hospital department because they actually have more time to see representatives there. You will find that many of your office based physicians will see not only their private patients in the private hospitals but they will also donate some of their time to see patients in the public system. This allows you to have at least three different site locations in which you may call on your targeted physicians.

Hospital Department Physician Calls

It is possible to see physicians and provide information in various formats in different departments. Some examples are:

Sales calls in hospital departments.

The sales call is conducted with either a single physician or a group of physicians.

In-services.

In-services are educational meetings set up to provide a more conducive environment for making sales presentations and for gaining quality presentation time with key physicians and key physician influencers.

During hospital in-services modest meals may be provided to insure that the physician has time to speak with you. This can't be "just a meal" for the physicians. You must present product information and this is a good time to show company approved product videos and to utilize clinical studies and other pertinent product data.

Video, Audio and Teleconferences.

Work with medical leaders. Video conferencing has gained favor over older types of learning programs such as teleconferences and audio conferences. Computer-based learning programs have been utilized for years now. Many hospitals enjoy having these educational programs for their physicians. This allows the physicians to earn CEUs, continuing education units, during a luncheon and there is no need for the physicians to take time off work. These programs are usually held in a conference room at the hospital. These "speaker programs" are set up so that physicians across the country can all attend without leaving their homes, offices, or hospitals. This can be especially helpful for the public hospital physicians.

Speaker Programs.

Speaker programs are educational programs arranged by the pharmaceutical sales representative and their company. A physician specialist who is an expert in a particular medical field will be paid a fee by the pharmaceutical company to speak to a group of targeted hospital physicians. This is set up just like a speaker program for office-based physicians. The difference is the hospital setting. The speaker should provide pertinent up-to-date information on the treatment and management of disease. He should not "push" one particular product or his credibility will be lost. Of course, when you choose a speaker for your educational program you will always choose a speaker who writes for, and approves of, your product. The whole idea behind speaker programs is to have an impartial expert give unbiased information to your physician audience that is favorable to your product.

Displays.

What is a "display?" Inside the hospital or at a different location, pharmaceutical sales reps use large visual product displays placed on top of tables which hold pharmaceutical products, clinical studies, and other visual aides. These items are used during product presentations to physicians. In general, hospitals who allow displays will set aside certain dates and times for pharmaceutical product displays. The representatives will schedule appointments as allowed and will work these displays on the designated days. Sometimes displays are the only approved means of seeing hospital based physicians and pharmacists.

Journal Club Meetings.

These meetings usually take place at the hospital and may take place very early in the morning. Usually, physicians in the group take turns presenting interesting cases or papers to the rest of the group. I was always amazed at the volume of research materials some physicians used and how well they prepared for these relatively informal physician group meetings. These meetings are held by physicians for physicians for the sole purpose of increasing their medical knowledge. Being invited to attend a meeting is quite an honor and should always be treated as such. You are their guest.

Outpatient Clinics.

These are clinics were patients in the public system go to a designated hospital area to be seen by physicians just as private patients are in the private clinic settings. These clinics are set up for hospital and on-going patient follow-up assessments. This can be a great place to see many key physicians as you work smart and tailor your presentations to this setting as well as to your physicians.

Physician's Lounge.

You enter this area by invitation only. Follow the lead and recommendations given by the physician who has invited you into the area.

CME Office.

All continuing education programs are usually set up through this Continuing Medical Education office.

Department Head Offices.

These very influential physicians are extremely valuable to you. In addition to being given the opportunity to influence the medical department heads, usually gaining access to these physicians creates access to other physicians within the hospital. These physicians also play a key role in influencing the P&T committee, especially since some of them will be on the committee.

Preceptorships with Influential Physicians.

Gaining permission from and spending a day with a key physician to observe his work is an outstanding achievement and a fantastic opportunity to develop rapport with an important physician and gain greater insight into his needs as a physician.

Grand Rounds.

This is an educational meeting where the Department Chief or some other physician speaks on a particular disease state, treatment stats, etc.

Resource allocation is a term you will hear over and over in the hospital. All hospital departments operate within a set budget and the needs of that department are analyzed and prioritized. The successful hospital sales representative becomes a partner, consultant and valuable team member within the department. **There is no room for average sales representatives who see their jobs as product presenters, doughnut and sample droppers and nothing more.**

Nursing Home Physician Calls

Another potential location for seeing your hard to see office based physician is the nursing home. Find out if your physician sees nursing home patients. If so, you would follow the same hospital rules for gathering information about seeing the physician at the nursing home. The most likely physician specialities making nursing home rounds would be geriatric specialists, internal medicine and general practitioners, especially in the smaller towns. Normally, your first point of contact when calling on a nursing home will be the director's office or the assistant director's office. Follow the rules here just as you would in any hospital or other institution.

What is the P&T Committee? What is their function?

The P&T Committee (Pharmacy and Therapeutics Committee) is a group normally comprised of 8-10 physician and pharmacist members who evaluate and vote on drugs to be added to or deleted from the hospital formulary. The hospital formulary list is a listing of all drugs approved by the committee and purchased by the pharmacy. Hospital prescribers may write prescriptions for inpatient and outpatient use and the pharmacy may dispense these drugs without any additional paperwork being submitted and without any delays.

If you have hospital responsibility and are responsible for gaining formulary acceptance, one of the most important physician groups that you must work with or influence will be those physicians on the Pharmacy and Therapeutics Committee.

Don't expect to see a list of physicians and pharmacists who are on the P&T Committee. This information is often a deeply guarded secret. Quite often, the Pharmacy and Therapeutics Committee member list is deliberately kept out of pharmaceutical sales representatives hands. This is done to prevent the sales representatives from targeting and having undue influence over a team of people who are required to act within set guidelines that meet patient treatment protocol and the pharmacy budget.

One of your greatest allies within the hospital will be your targeted department head. For example, if you sell a product that provides treatment for MI (myocardial infarction) patients then the head of cardiology is a major target for you. He may or may not be on the P&T committee and you may or may not know this. Either way, he will be very influential in the decision making process dictating whether your product is added to the hospital formulary. After you determine that you have the support of this specialist for your product, ask for the physician's help with gaining formulary acceptance for your product. If you truly have his support you should not have difficulty gaining a commitment from the physician to speak to the P&T Committee.

Example: From day one when I was hired as a pharmaceutical sales representative I had heavy hospital call responsibility because of the concentration of important Veterans Administration Hospitals and other public hospitals within my territory. The medical specialist didn't work in these hospitals at all; the responsibility was mine. I soon learned to cultivate support from key physicians and to assist them in their efforts to place my products on their hospital formularies. I have done everything from gathering competitor's data along with hospital outcomes data through the pharmacy to prepare cost-effective analysis documents to support the addition of my products to the formulary; to writing and preparing power point presentations for my pharmacy directors and key physician specialists to use for their presentations to the formulary committee meetings. My product formulary success rate was very high because I targeted the right people and I made my physician and pharmacist allies jobs of pushing my product easy.

If you don't take anything else from this book, take the following thought:

You are only one person, therefore you are limited in the number of places you can be at any given time on any given day. Your ultimate success will result from your sales recruitment effort. You must recruit your own sales force so the more physicians, pharmacists and healthcare professionals you recruit to sell your product, the more product you will sell. The best sales representatives are those who work smart.

While you can apply office-based sales techniques to many hospital and nursing home departments, there is one special hospital department where you need additional understanding of the department itself in order to call on the department physicians successfully. For that reason I am supplying additional information on the Emergency Medicine Department.

How do you sell in the emergency medicine department?

First of all, there are varying sizes of emergency medicine departments. Different emergency medicine departments may see 10,000-100,000 patients per year based on hospital size, type, and location.

Emergency medicine departments are categorized based on their treatment options. They are:

a. Level I
   Small, rural hospital with one physician or physician's assistant providing coverage in time blocks.

b. Level II
   Has 24 hour physician coverage. Other physician specialties are on-call and must show up within one hour of being called.

c. Level III
Has 24 hour physician coverage with all hospital departments fully covered. These are full trauma centers and are frequently teaching hospitals.

Emergency medicine physicians are some of the best trained physicians in the medical field. They must know many medical specialty areas well in order to practice effectively in the Emergency Medicine Department. Think about it. They must know neurology, psychiatry, obstetrics, cardiology, endocrinology, plastic surgery, etc. Their knowledge of pharmaceutical products must be just as extensive because they are practicing in numerous specialty fields all day long, every day. That means no matter which product you are promoting, you have found key physicians here who need to know about your products and how to write them.

There are certain major areas of concentration regarding the Emergency Medicine Department function and layout. They are:

1. Drug Therapy: for all types of patients and all types of disease states and injuries.
2. Trauma: area devoted to treating trauma injuries.
3. Poison: area devoted to treatment of accidental and deliberate poisonings including prescription drug overdoses.
4. Internal Medicine: handling of all types of illnesses.
5. Critical Care: for the treatment of all patients with life threatening medical disease or trauma.

Most emergency medicine departments are "closed" departments. This means that no provision has been made for "visits" by pharmaceutical sales representatives.

Your goal should be twofold:

1. Sell to physicians in this very stressful environment.

   A. Choose your time carefully. Never attempt to speak with a busy physician, PA or nurse. You will defeat your purpose if you try to speak with them when they are busy. This would show a lack of respect on your part for them and the patient. Ask for time when you see that they are not busy. Present information only after you have gained permission to do so. You can't force people to give you time or to be receptive to your message. When you show them that you do respect their time and that you are a professional, you will be treated as one.

   B. Know about product access restrictions before you speak with the physician. Know whether the patients will be able to fill their prescriptions at the hospital pharmacy before leaving and whether they will have difficulty filling the script at pharmacies outside the hospital. If the patient will have difficulty filling their prescription outside the hospital, you must have a plan going in to make it easy for the physician to write the prescription for the patient and for the patient to fill the prescription. Have appropriate prior authorization forms with you and a list of area pharmacies stocking your product.

2. Do not interfere with patient treatment.

An excellent journal to read to gain understanding of the emergency medicine department is *The Journal of Emergency Medicine*. You may also look into the local chapter of the Emergency Department Nurses Association. They will have regular meetings that you can attend and support with permission. Being known and valued by the nurses will help you go far in this department.

Part

3

Your ultimate success will result from your sales recruitment effort.

Chapter 8

Selling to Pharmacists

In addition to calling on office-based physicians, it is vital that you call on independent pharmacists, pharmacy directors, hospital, clinical and institutional pharmacists.

Who are these often neglected professionals who are absolutely critical to your selling success? What part do they play in script writing, hospital, institution, physician and patient influence? Why is it very important to provide the same information to pharmacists that you provide to your physicians? How do you get time with these important people? While they are typically easier to see than physicians, you must provide value added service to pharmacists and never waste their time if you hope to create positive, win-win relationships with your pharmacists. This chapter will address these questions and more.

What is the pharmacist's job description?

We all know that pharmacists fill prescriptions written by physicians, but they do so much more. Pharmacists are experts on drugs and they have very important patient management and consultative responsibilities because of their expertise in the field of pharmacology.

The passage of OBRA helped define and describe the pharmacist's job description.

OBRA: Omnibus Budget Reconciliation Act
Passed in 1990

The passage of this act required that pharmacists perform drug utilization reviews and document patient counseling. Starting in the year 2002, pharmacists must complete a six year degree program which results in a Pharm. D. Degree. Many specialize in certain types of pharmacy work and may attend postgraduate residency programs to achieve specific certifications in such areas as compounding.

Pharmacists are responsible for keeping patients' prescription history along with other health information such as drug allergies in order to monitor patients' drug therapy for maximum benefit and the reduction of potential drug interactions and allergic reactions.

Pharmacists perform their jobs by following the OBRA job description outline. The general outline follows:

Drug Utilization Review

Part 1: Therapeutic

Appropriate therapeutic usage
Utilization
Duplication
Drug contraindications
Drug interactions
Drug allergies
Clinical misuse

Part 2: Patient Consultation

Complete patient identification information
Complete patient drug-related history
Complete medication administration information
Common side effects, adverse effects, interactions and
complications with recommended actions in the event
they occur.

What part do they play in script writing, hospital,
institution, physician and patient influence?

Pharmacists discuss patients' drug therapy with physicians
numerous times every day. Collaboration between
pharmacists and physicians is very common now.
Pharmacists make recommendations to the physicians
based on other drug therapy, drug interactions, patient
health conditions and drug therapy cost. Pharmacists are
often able to make suggestions for drug consolidations to
treat more than one illness saving the patient money and
reducing the chance for drug to drug interactions. As the
pharmacists make more and more suggestions for certain
drugs and treatment regimens that the physicians utilize

in their patient care, the more comfortable physicians become using certain drugs or categories of drugs for their patients. Soon physician writing habits are established. Once they are established, they are not easily changed. It is easy to see why the successful pharmaceutical sales representative typically has an entire "team" of pharmacists selling products for her 24/7.

Now pharmacists provide a newer more intensive type of patient counseling known as Medication Therapy Management. This is especially useful in community pharmacies. Basically, the pharmacist offers special intensive counseling to targeted medicare patients with multiple chronic disease states who are taking multiple medications and incurring large medication expenses. The goal is to consolidate drugs wherever possible to treat more than one disease state and in some cases change drug therapies or even eliminate them if there is duplication of medication treatments.

Why is it very important to provide the same information to pharmacists that you provide to your physicians? The pharmacist needs the same information that the physician needs and it is critical to the sales representative's success to treat the pharmacists as "physician equals."

Sales Calls on Pharmacists of all types should include:

Product and Formulary Information.

Provide your pharmacists with product, formulary, rebate, patient, and pharmacy education information (for other pharmacists) along with books, pens, pads and any other useful items you may have. With retail pharmacists you are typically making a one-on-one sales presentation and answering questions just as you would with a physician. You will present information to individual pharmacists in hospitals or institutions the same way.

In-service or Training Sessions.

In-services are typically performed with large groups of pharmacists in clinics, hospitals and nursing homes. In a hospital or institutional pharmacy, the in-service will be like a physician group in-service and you may provide a meal or snacks for the pharmacists. Normally, you will invite key pharmacists to all hospital physician speaker programs and treat them as you would any physician.

Regular pharmacy call cycles.

Pharmacy calls should be based on the pharmacist's time schedule, area of influence and pharmacist's needs.

How do you get time with these important people?

During your initial pharmacy call, you will introduce yourself, meet as many pharmacists and assistants as possible, find out which days and times are best for making calls on their department and what their educational needs are. Find out any additional information that you need to know to make your calls on your pharmacists more productive based on the type of pharmacy department and the individual pharmacist's needs.

The key to gaining quality time with any pharmacist is the same as with any physician. You must always have important helpful information to share and never waste the pharmacist's time.

Retail Pharmacists.

Independents and Chains are pharmacies who are owned and operated independently by a pharmacist or pharmacy chains such as CVS, Walgreens, Rite Aid and others owned by companies or corporations.

Why do you need to call on independent pharmacists and those who work in chains, especially with the proliferation of managed care formularies?

Managed care formularies are very often complex formularies with many unclear restrictions and exceptions. The pharmacists very often function as the "go between" for the physician and the formulary. The pharmacist can influence the formulary drug list as well as the physician and can be of tremendous assistance to everyone involved with obtaining prior authorizations.

With the different tiered benefit plans, the pharmacists have a direct effect on which drugs are prescribed and on which scripts the patients decide to fill.

Pharmacists provide a fount of useful information about how insurance companies process scripts for your product and how patients and physicians respond to the process and the medication.

A primary concern for independent pharmacies is the competition from chains. Independents tend to utilize patient education resources because they have more personal relationships with their customers. Always respect the pharmacists' time. Find out the best time to call on them and then do so.

Collaborate with your pharmacists to provide community education programs. For example if you sell respiratory products, you may be able to schedule a health screening program at your local pharmacy. You could coordinate the program with the respiratory therapy department from your hospital. The respiratory therapists could perform pulmonary function testing and give patients test results to take to their physicians. The pharmacists could provide counseling to patients already on respiratory drugs. If available, you could also pass out spacers to be used with inhalers along with patient instruction pamphlets.

The idea is to create a win-win situation for all parties. Everyone should benefit from this coordinated healthcare screening, especially the patients. The same type program or variations can be held at nursing homes, clinic pharmacies and in hospital pharmacies, respiratory therapy departments, etc.

Your success with pharmacists will be determined by how well you provide the services that the individual pharmacies need. This is the same underlying principle that you will employ when calling on physicians. You must always individualize your sales calls regardless of who your customer is at that time. "Cookie cutter" calls have long since lost their appeal and their effectiveness.

Federal regulations such as the Health Insurance Portability and Accountability Act (HIPPA) made pharmacy calls more challenging so pharmaceutical sales representatives became more creative in order to perform well at their jobs. HIPPA rules protect patient privacy and affect how much information the pharmacists may provide to pharmaceutical sales representatives.

Clinical Pharmacists.

Clinical pharmacist includes all pharmacists working in hospitals, clinics and other institutions. I find this term to be misleading. Understanding the different types of pharmacists within an institution such as a hospital may be challenging at first. For that reason I will explain the different types of pharmacists you may find in the following institutions/departments. Within each pharmacy department you will find further specialization of pharmacy duties. With hospitals in particular you will find pharmacists working in designated specialty areas.

Hospital Pharmacy Department.

Pharmacy Director

The pharmacy director is directly responsible for the actions of the entire pharmacy department just as the medical director is responsible for physicians and others who report to him in the department. The director's position is very much a business position and the pharmacy director is responsible for preparing, submitting and gaining approval for the pharmacy budget. The role is primarily an administrative one and an important one because the director's decisions about whether or not sales representatives are allowed into the pharmacy and under what conditions is usually at his sole discretion. Some directors enjoy staying on top of new information and are interested in all clinical studies while others may not devote as much time to this area, deferring almost entirely to the clinical pharmacist(s) for needed information and updates.

Clinical Pharmacist

It is not possible to over-emphasize the importance of this person! If you could name only one person in the pharmacy whom you need on your side in order to be a successful pharmaceutical sales representative, it would be the hospital clinical pharmacist.

Clinical pharmacists are directly involved with prescribing drugs for patients. They review charts, make drug prescription recommendations, perform drug utilization reviews, coordinate the pharmacy part of in-hospital drug studies, perform research and prepare drug study results for the medical staff and formulary committees. They make presentations and recommendations to formulary committees and are often one of the formulary committee members. It is the clinical pharmacist who collaborates with physicians about patient prescriptions the most, although all pharmacists do this to differing degrees.

Successful hospital sales depends on your ability to gain formulary acceptance for your product. The best place to gain information and start the approval process is to collaborate with your clinical pharmacist and work with this person to do whatever you need to do within the confines of your company's rules and regulations to gain formulary acceptance for your products.

Staff Pharmacists

These hospital/institutional pharmacists are basically the equivalent of retail pharmacists and they typically handle the routine pharmacist duties such as filling prescriptions, checking for drug to drug interactions and counseling patients.

Nursing Homes/Institutions.

It is not uncommon for clinical pharmacists or groups of compounding pharmacists to provide services to nursing homes and other extended care facilities. You must find out which type of pharmacist you are calling on in every situation and then adjust your sales call to meet that pharmacist's needs.

The opportunity for volume sales is great in these institutions as it is in hospitals. For example, if you sell an excellent antihypertensive drug that is extremely effective overall, has a low incidence of side effects, is cost effective and is easily dosed, you have an opportunity to convert most if not all of the hypertensive patients in the institution to your drug.

Pharmacy Consultants.

Sometimes pharmacy consultants work strictly in that capacity for pharmacy groups and for institutions. They oversee quality assurance programs and quality control programs. These pharmacists are typically pharmacists with advanced degrees and expertise in these areas. They are highly influential in establishing formularies in institutions.

Community Projects.

Health Fairs

As stated previously, health fairs present fantastic opportunities to establish rapport with pharmacists and other key healthcare personnel. By participating in health fairs you gain good exposure for your company and products.

This also helps set you apart from those sales representatives who perform at the minimum level rather than the maximum level possible.

Patient Education and Testing

Providing patient education materials and free testing whenever possible is a great community service that should be provided by you and your company whenever possible. After all, if you have great products that provide effective treatment for disease states the more people you can educate and influence, the more "sales representatives" you will effectively recruit to assist your sales efforts.

Additionally, providing patient education materials to all pharmacists saves tremendous time for busy pharmacists who are attempting to fill prescriptions, keep up all of their paperwork, consult with physicians, counsel patients and answer patient questions.

More and more efforts are being made to recognize and classify pharmacists as healthcare providers.

If the sales representative remembers one thing as most important in all sales calls, it is to provide accurate and complete product information to all customers so that sound decisions can be made when choosing pharmacological agents for the treatment of disease states.

Chapter 9

Managed Care

What is a Managed Care Organization (MCO)? It is a company that provides medical services to its members. Some examples of MCOs are:

- Aetna
- Blue Cross
- Cigna

The MCO will contract with health care providers such as physicians and hospitals, to provide medical services to its members. A list of the "Participating Providers," physicians and hospitals that they have contracted with for services, are then made available to the managed care organization members.

What is a formulary? A formulary is a listing of medications approved by the MCO for use by and reimbursement of the MCO members or providers. A formulary may include a list of generic and brand drugs. Generics are chemically equivalent products for branded prescription drugs who have lost their patents. However, generics cost less than branded drugs because they consist of the active drug plus some inactive filler and do not generally consist of 100% active drug as branded drugs do.

MCOs have different types of formularies. These formularies are:

- Open. In an open system, all drugs are covered.

- Closed. Only drugs on the formulary are allowed to be dispensed by the pharmacy. This is usually controlled by NDC Blockout. An NDC Blockout allows the terminal used by the pharmacist to seek payment approval from the MCO for a medication to block payment by the MCO for non-approved drugs.

- Mixed. Employees may have access to all medications on the formulary. Usually a co-pay is required. A co-pay is a payment that the member makes when utilizing an MCO service. There are different types of co-pays. In a Two Tiered Co-Pay System, the member may pay $5.00 for generic product versus $15.00 for a branded formulary product. In a Three Tiered Co-Pay System, one co-pay price is set for the generic drug, another price is set for the branded on-formulary drug, and another price is set for the non-formulary drug. These co-pays may cost the patient $10

$20/$30 respectively. These tiered co-pay amounts are meant to control the distribution of medications. Sometimes one class of medications will be open and one class will be closed.

What is a PBM? A Pharmacy Benefit Manager is a company that manages drug benefits for a managed care plan. They issue a prescription card to the patient, reimburse the pharmacy for the cost of the drug plus the filing fee, less co-pay amounts and bill the MCO for the balance.

Other Insurance Plans:

Medicare: A federally funded health insurance primarily for the elderly (65 years and older) and the disabled.
- Part A: Covers hospital, long-term and home health care and in hospital medications.
- Part B: Covers physician services, lab tests, EKGs, X-Rays, etc.

Medicaid: A federally funded program administered by states to provide medical benefits to low income individuals.

Forms of MCOs:

- PPO: Preferred Provider Organization provides a discounted fee structure, normally a FFS (Fee For Service) or a prepaid capitated fee in exchange for granting a provider "Preferred" status in treating the group's members.

- POS: Point of Service is a system that allows the member to choose between an HMO, PPO, or

Indemnity Coverage when treatment is needed rather than forcing the member to make a commitment for healthcare treatment during the enrollment process. Going outside the network is allowed but additional fees are charged to the member.

- IPAs: Individual Practice Associations is a form of HMO where the physicians see the HMO members in their private offices. This allows the physician to see private pay patients along with the HMO patients.

- Network Model: This is an IPA of group practices. The physician groups see HMO patients as well as private pay patients in their offices.

- Staff Model: MCOs hire physicians as salaried employees. The physicians operate out of their offices but they are employees of the MCO and usually have no private pay patients.

- Group Model: The MCO contracts with a group of physicians and pays the physicians a set amount per patient to provide a set of services based on a contract.

- ISN: Integrated Service Network offers hospital care, physician services, etc. under one plan.

Contract Models:

- Fee For Service (FFS): Pays providers a specific fee for service on each service they provide to a patient. This type of model encourages:

  A. Over-treatment of Patients. The more tests, procedures and office visits the physician orders the greater his reimbursement.

  B. Expensive Care Over Less Expensive Care. Physicians are paid more for ordering expensive tests, performing surgery, etc. rather than prescribing a drug that may treat the patient's illness effectively.

  C. Poor patient care. Failure to properly diagnose and treat the patient the first time results in increased visits for the patient. This is financially rewarding for the physician.

  Because of the high probability of abuse, direct fee reimbursement is rare. The MCO will generally contract with a group and that group is responsible for monitoring it's members.

- Case Rates. Under this type of contract, the provider agrees to service patients under an all-inclusive amount based on the disease or procedure. The physician has incentive to make the right diagnosis the first time and treat the patient effectively.

- Capitation. Typically, the HMOs are the most common MCOs to use capitation. The physician is paid a set amount per month for every member in the plan. Capitation offers strict control and does not encourage scheduling patient visits. The physician has incentive to make the right diagnosis the first time and treat the patient effectively.

These capitated contracts will be structured as:

> 1. Global risk. Global risk means the physician will be financially responsible for all healthcare services including and not limited to hospital services, physician services, pharmacy, etc.
> 2. Full Professional Risk. Here the physician will be financially responsible for hospital services and physician services.
> 3. Professional Risk. The physician is only financially responsible for physician services.

MCO physicians will be responsible for three components when they are capitated. These are:

- Hospital costs.
- Physician costs.
- Ancillary costs.

How MCOs affect pharmaceutical sales representative responsibilities:

When the MCO restricts which medication the physician can write for his patient this has a tremendous impact on the pharmaceutical sales representative's ability to do their job. Branded products are much more expensive than generic products and MCOs focus on controlling costs. This makes getting a more expensive product on formulary very difficult. In order to get products placed on an MCOs formulary, the MCO requires that there be a demonstrated demand for the product before they will consider the product for placement on the formulary. This means that physicians must write up prior authorizations and submit them to the MCO for approval.

The pharmaceutical sales representative must keep in mind the information that we have covered. Primarily, the sales representative needs to remember that only 15% of the capitated dollar will be spent on pharmaceutical products. In order for the sales representative to promote her product successfully, she must be able to show the physician how her product will reduce some of the high-cost capitated treatment areas for the physician. Specifically, the sales representative must focus on how her product will help reduce patient care costs, such as hospital stays, emergency room visits, office visits, laboratory testing and procedures. Pharmaceutical sales representatives can no longer be successful with the standard sales message. The new message must be expanded to include the financial benefits to the MCO physician.

Disease Management Programs offered by pharmaceutical companies prove very beneficial selling tools. This adds to the total cost-effectiveness of using your company's products.

Prior Authorization:

When a medication is not on the formulary of an MCO, a physician may write a prescription for a patient participant in the plan by following strict rules. The physician must fill out a form called the Prior Authorization Form. This is a form requesting that a prescription for the non-formulary medication be approved. In order to fill out this form, the physician must have good reasons for going outside the current formulary list of medications. Some of those reasons are:

- Patient is allergic to the formulary medication.
- Patient has been treated with all formulary meds for current condition and the treatment was ineffective.
- Patient requires additional treatment along with the formulary medication in order to achieve an efficacious result.
- New medication has significantly better efficacy as compared to older medications with better side effect profiles. The end result is that the overall cost of patient treatment is reduced because better efficacy and a lower incidence of side effects mean fewer physician visits, reduced hospitalizations and less overall treatment complications.

How do you get the Physician to fill out the Prior Authorization Form?

- First, you should identify your largest writers of prescriptions in your territory. You can do this using company supplied information. Next, look at your territory health care market information. See which MCOs your best prescribers belong to before proceeding. Do a pre-call analysis on each physician. Is the physician capitated or are most of his patients enrolled in a FFS plan? Does he follow the health plan formularies? Is he a member of the P&T Committee? If so, pass this information along to your Managed Care Specialist. Develop a sales strategy for each key physician based on his needs.

- Second, you must convince the physician that your product is worth his time and effort to write prior authorizations. You must sell him on your product. Ask for the business! Gain a commitment.

- Third, you must sell him on the benefits of prescribing your product within the MCO system. In order to do this, you must convince him that the following will result:

   1. Reduced patient office visits.
   2. Improved patient compliance.
   3. Emergency medicine visit reduction.
   4. Reduced cost to the patient.
   5. Reduced risks for the patient.
   6. Reduced treatment risks for the physician.
   7. Reduced physician time.

- Supply information. Be certain that the physician has a list of plans that require a Prior Authorization for your product.

- Supply information on proper submission procedures for prior authorization. Usually Prior Authorization Forms are faxed or telephoned in to the MCO by the physician's office. All pertinent identifying information must be included on the form. Each HMO will have an approved Prior Authorization Form. If the physician office does not have one they can request that the HMO fax them one for their use.

- Know the correct "key words" to use on the Prior Authorization form to increase the physician's chance of getting the Prior Authorization accepted. Your Managed Care Specialist within your company will have this information. This should be supplied to the general sales force and any sales force dealing with managed care physicians.

- Let the physician know that he is not alone! Be certain that he knows that other physicians are also writing prior authorizations. Always get permission from the physician who is writing the prior authorization to share this information with others. An individual physician who goes against the HMO to write outside the formulary will soon suffer the consequences of his actions, but large numbers of physicians writing outside the formulary will place pressure on the HMO to add the product to the formulary.

- Find out if there are other individuals, within the physician's office, who handle Prior Authorizations. Sometimes one designated person does this. It may be a nurse, nurse practitioner or a PA. Work with that person wherever practical.

- Always show support for those physicians who go above and beyond to write your products! All physicians will not do this. In addition to the "thank you" give these physicians the very best service they have ever had from any representative. They deserve it!

How do MCOs get physicians to write the formulary drugs and reduce the number of Prior Authorizations?

Bonuses. The physicians are rewarded by the MCO for writing medications that are formulary approved. If they write only formulary medications, they get a full bonus. If they write 5% of non-formulary medications, their bonus may be reduced 20%. The more non-formulary medications the physician writes, the less money he will make! That hardly seems fair. In effect, the physician is being punished for placing his patient's welfare first.

- DURs: Drug Utilization Reviews measure the physicians writing habits for particular disease states. These results are measured against approved treatment algorithms. Failing to comply with the MCOs preferred methods of treatment for disease states regardless of the individual patient's case, will cause the physician to get reprimanded. If the physician continues to go against the HMO he can be dropped.

How does the representative arm herself with knowledge about the managed care market and specifically how it affects her territory?

- Find out if there are any national managed care organizations based in your area (example: California).

- Find out how many large corporations are based in your area. They tend to use HMOs for medical care plans.

- Are there large groups of physicians or physicians/ hospital groups?

- Communicate with the managed care representative covering your territory to learn specifics about managed care in your territory and at the state level.

- Find out the population demographics in your area. Having specific groups such as large numbers of elderly people (example: Florida) will alert you to the type of MCO operating in your area.

Most physicians will operate under a fee-for-service contract but as many as 25% of your physicians may be capitated in some areas.

Conclusion

Congratulations on your many accomplishments thus far! You have excelled in order to reach a place where you would read books such as mine to assist you in your pharmaceutical sales efforts. Your chosen career is a great one and I know you will truly enjoy knowing that you have made a positive impact on the lives of many other people.

I hope you have found the information in this book beneficial and that you will use it to perform to your best ability. I know that you will learn many new ways to succeed at your job on your own, in addition to the ideas and suggestions that I have made based on my own personal experience working in various positions within the pharmaceutical industry.

Good Selling!

Jane Williams

Part

4

It's virtually impossible to overcome an opponent who won't give up.

Resources

Academy of Managed Care Pharmacy
   http://www.amcp.org/

American Pharmacists Association
   http://www.aphanet.org

American Society of Health-System Pharmacists
   http://www.ashp.org/

Emergency Medicine
   http://www.emedmag.com/

Food and Drug Administration
   http://www.fda.gov/

Managed Care Magazine
   http://www.managedcaremag.com/

Nursing World
   http://www.nursingworld.org/

Pharmaceutical/Biotechnology Companies
   http://www.samford.edu/schools/pharmacy/
   dic/pharmcomp.htm

Pharmaceutical Company Links
   http://www.pharmacy.org/company.html

Pharmaceutical Representative Magazine
http://www.pharmrep.com

Pharmaceutical Research and Manufacturers
of America- PhRMA
http://www.phrma.org/

Pharmacists
http://www.bls.gov/oco/ocos079.htm

SEMPA- Society of Emergency Medicine
Physicians Assistants
http://www.sempa.org/

The Journal of the American Medical
Association- JAMA
http://jama.ama-assn.org/

The New England Journal of Medicine
http://content.nejm.org/

Index

A

Accessing Performance 35
Adult Learner 37
Adult Personality 39
Advanced Sales Classes 21

B

Basic Sales Presentation 48

C

Call Frequency 25
Call Planner 24
Calling On Physicians 64
Capitation 106
Clinical Pharmacists 96, 97, 98
Close 56
CME Office 79
Consultative Selling 62
Contract Models 105
Co-Promotion 34

D

Department Head Offices 79
Dinner/Lunch Speaker Programs 31
Displays 67, 77
District Meetings 30
Dramatizing Your Message 52
Drug Utilization Review 91, 111

E

Educational Meetings 30, 33
Emergency Medicine 83, 84, 86

F

Feeler 39
Formulary 32, 102

G

Gatekeeper 65
Grand Rounds 79
Group Model 104

H

Handling Objections 55
Health Fairs 98
Health Insurance Portability and Accountability Act 95
HMO 103, 110
Home Study 19
Hospital In-services 67
Hospital Specialists 69

I

IPAs 104
Initial Training 20
In-service Programs 66, 67, 92
Internship 44
Intuitor 40
Integrated Service Network 104

J

Journal Club Meetings 31, 66, 78

L

Learning Programs 33
Listening 50

M

Medical Journals 27
Medical Library 27
Medical Research 26
Medical Society Meetings 31
Managed Care 94, 101
Managed Care Organization 101
Managed Care Specialist 110
MCO 101, 110-112
Medicaid 103
Medicare 103

N

National Meetings 29
Network Model 104
Nursing Home 80

O

OBRA 90
Outpatient Clinics 78

P

Patient Consultation 91, 98
Patient Education and Testing 99
Performance Meetings 30
Pharmacies 94
Pharmacists 89, 90, 92, 94, 95, 99
Pharmacy 93
Pharmacy consultants 98
Pharmacy Director 89, 96
PhRMA 61
Physician Access 75
Physician Door Openers 66
Physician's Lounge 79
POA Meetings 29
POS 103
PPO 103
Preceptorships 79

Presenting 51
President's Club/Circle Meetings 30
Prior Authorization 108, 109, 110, 111
Private Hospitals 70
Probing 53
Product and Formulary Information 92
Product Presentations 22
Proof Source 23
Public Hospitals 71
P&T Committee 80, 81

R

Regional/Bi-Regional Meetings 29
Relationship Selling 61
Residency 44

S

Safety 17
Sales Meetings 20
Sales Workshops 20
Sensor 40
Speaker Programs 66, 67, 77
Staff Model 104
Staff Pharmacists 97
Successful Selling 47
Supporting 54

T

Territory Analysis 24
Thinker 39
Time Management Skills 16

V

Veterans Affairs Hospitals 71
Video and Teleconferences 67

Printed in the United States
70914LV00002B/23